# READING to some PURPOSE

Ronald Ridout

BOOK 7

Oliver & Boyd

*Illustrated by Toni Goffe*

**Oliver & Boyd**
Robert Stevenson House
1–3 Baxter's Place
Leith Walk
Edinburgh EH1 3BB

*A Division of Longman Group Ltd*

ISBN 0 05 003475 8

First published 1959
Second edition 1982

Printed in Hong Kong by
Wilture Enterprise (International) Ltd

# PREFACE

The seven books of *Reading to Some Purpose* provide a complete training in reading thoughtfully. More specifically, they train the children to read for interpretation, selection and accuracy, for comparison, implication and appreciation, for speed, for bias and discrimination. The long-range aim is to prepare the pupil to be able to read intelligently in adult life.

The material used has been selected with an eye to the children's interests at their own level of reading; yet it is broad enough to include stories, descriptions, expositions, dialogue, verse, indexes, dictionaries, diagrams, graphs, tables and maps.

A subsidiary purpose of *Reading to Some Purpose* is to train children from the outset how to write down their findings. It is not assumed that this ability just comes with a little practice. A great variety of devices is used to ensure that the children will in fact write well-constructed English. In many instances the work is set in such a way that they cannot help but write the correct answers, for children learn by doing, but they learn more surely by doing correctly.

The books have been carefully graded by control of vocabulary, sentence structure, idiom, and comprehension difficulties, according to reading age. Books 1–4 are graded to provide work for half a year each; Books 5–7 have sufficient work for one year each. The choice of content, layout, and presentation ensure that all pupils may work from books appropriate to their interests and levels of attainment.

*Reading to Some Purpose* can be used for class, group, or individual work. The minimum amount of guidance from the teacher is required.

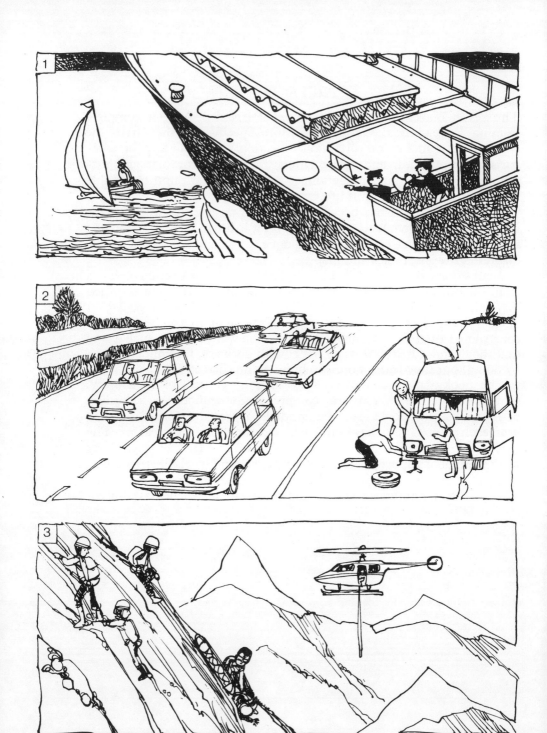

# Unit 1 What's Happening?

1. Look at the pictures on the opposite page. Write 1, 2, 3, in your book and beside each write a title for the picture.
   Choose from:
   Collision Course
   Breakdown
   Mountain Rescue

2. Look at picture 1. Write answers to these questions.
   Write complete sentences.
   (a) How many people can you see on the oil tanker?
   (b) Have they seen the sailing boat?
   (c) Has the man in the sailing boat seen the oil tanker?

3. Look at picture 2. Answer the questions:
   (a) How many cars can you see in the picture?
   (b) What has happened to the broken-down car?
   (c) How many people were travelling in the car?

4. Now look at picture 3 and answer the questions:
   (a) What do you think has happened?
   (b) Has the helicopter lowered a stretcher?
   (c) How many climbers were on the mountain?

# Unit 2 An Exciting Ride

The stirrups were miles too long for my legs, but that helped me to mount. Once up, I crossed them noiselessly – this wasn't the moment to fiddle with leathers! I could see the lane through the wood a few yards away and, in the direction of the Saddle track, the gap in the trees where it ended. Would there be a big gate or stile? I'd have to chance it. Another terrific roll of thunder shook the whole wood. I kicked my heels into the Arab pony's flanks and she went straight into a gallop, almost leaving me seated in the air. But I clung to the front arch of the saddle and from that moment I was too thrilled to give a thought to lurking Spiros, bullets whistling from behind or any other dangers.

From *Friday's Tunnel* by John Verney

1. Read the passage and make a list of all the words connected with horses.
2. How do you know the girl is trying to be quiet?
3. What sort of danger might she be in?
4. What do you think she might do if there was a big gate or stile?
5. Is it night or day? How do you know?

# Unit 3  Choose the Meaning

Choose the correct words from the brackets and write out the complete sentences.

1. To keep fit means (to fit exactly, to keep in good health).
2. A musician is (a person who plays music, a person who can act).
3. A bookworm is (a grub that eats paper, a person very fond of books).
4. To pull one's weight means (to drag weights along, to do one's best).
5. To strike while the iron is hot means (to seize one's chance, to do one's ironing early).
6. A tricycle is (a practice cycle, a bicycle, a cycle with three wheels).
7. To lose one's temper means (to lose one's way, to become angry, to mislay one's matches).
8. If all your fingers are thumbs you are feeling (ill, dishonest, clumsy, lazy).

Now write a sentence explaining each of the following words and phrases.  *Begin like this:*

9. A helicopter is an aeroplane with the airscrew overhead.

9. A helicopter is . . .
10. A hovercraft . . .
11. An audience . . .
12. A dictionary . . .
13. To lose one's head means . . .
14. To talk through one's hat . . .
15. Look before you leap . . .
16. To get cold feet . . .

# Unit 4 Draw the Picture

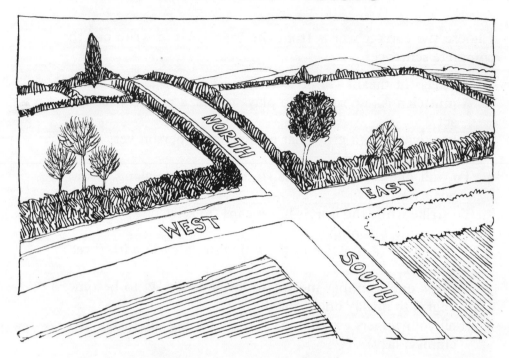

This is a picture of crossroads just outside a town. Copy it into your book, but make it much bigger. Then add to your picture, so that it shows all the following items quite clearly in their right places.

1. If you walk along the road to the west, there is a fence on the left-hand side.
2. In the south-west corner of the crossroads there is a signpost.
3. This signpost clearly shows that the road to the east goes to London, while the road to the west leads to Guildford.
4. In the field to the south-east there are two cows grazing.
5. There is a gate into this field through a hedge. The gate is half way along the road to the east.
6. The tops of churches and other tall buildings of a town are just visible over the hill to the north-east.

# Unit 5 Definitions

**equal:** well-balanced, the same in number
**inflammable:** easily catching fire
**cold-blooded:** deliberately cruel
**purchase:** to buy
**flavour:** the way something tastes
**arrogant:** too proud; conceited
**vandal:** someone who destroys things out of spite

Look at these definitions and then try to answer each of the following questions with a complete sentence.

1. If Jim left his rabbit hungry in a cold-blooded way, do you think he meant to do it or not?

2. If Mum decided to purchase a new TV set, would she buy it or rent it?

3. In football, two equal teams play against each other. Does each team have the same number of players?

4. If oil is very inflammable, is it likely to catch fire easily?

5. Sara doesn't like the flavour of strawberry ice-cream. Does that mean she enjoys the taste?

6. The successful pop star was very arrogant. Was he very humble or very proud?

7. A gang of vandals broke into the art gallery. Would they be likely to enjoy looking at the paintings or spoiling them?

# Unit 6 Christmas One Hundred Years Ago

Here are some statements about Christmas one hundred years ago. Five of them are true and five of them are untrue. The remaining four may or may not be true – you cannot tell because the story does not say. Read the story opposite, then write the statements in three groups headed:

     1. True     2. Untrue     3. May be True

Before Queen Victoria's reign, no children hung up stockings on Christmas Eve.

Children in Victorian times were not given any presents at Christmas.

The Victorians invented Christmas cards.

Children's parties in Victorian times were quite small.

At the Christmas parties children played noisy games.

People decorated their houses with holly and mistletoe.

Many poor people worked on Christmas Day.

The Mummers were professional actors.

These actors would move around their area at Christmas.

For the play they acted they wore their everyday clothes.

The play was about people in the village.

The Knight in the play came from Turkey.

The audience enjoyed the play.

Queen Victoria did not enjoy Christmas.

Presents were an important part of Christmas for well-to-do children. It was the Victorians who first began the custom of hanging their stockings on the bed post on Christmas Eve. For them there was also the fun of children's parties. Their parties were usually large and boisterous with dozens of excited children rushing about playing hunt-the-slipper and musical chairs.

In some villages a team of amateur actors called Mummers visited the manor house and farm houses wearing strange costumes and make-up. They would act a play about St George and the Turkish Knight. Everyone knew the play, but they never grew tired of seeing it again, and a visit from the Mummers was one of the big excitements of Christmas.

From *Victorian Children* by Eleanor Allen

# Unit 7 An Unknown Terror

I shall never forget the first train that ran by. I was feeding quietly near the fence which separated the meadow from the railway, when I heard a strange sound in the distance. Before I knew whence it came, with a rush and a clatter and a puffing out of smoke, a long black train of something flew by, and was gone almost before I could draw my breath. I turned and galloped to the further side of the meadow as fast as I could go, and there I stood snorting with astonishment and fear.

In the course of the day many other trains went by. For the first few days I could not feed in peace; but as I found that this terrible creature never came into the field or did me any harm, I began to disregard it. Very soon I cared as little about the passing of a train as the cows and sheep did.

From *Black Beauty* by Anna Sewell


Read this extract carefully and then complete the following sentences.

1. The meadow was separated from the railway by ...
2. Black Beauty snorted with astonishment and fear because ...
3. When the first train came past, Black Beauty was eating grass near ...
4. He galloped to the other side of the field when ...
5. He began to ignore the train because ...
6. I began to realise that it was a horse telling the story when ...
7. The first paragraph is about ...
8. The second paragraph tells how ...

# Unit 8  Which Meaning?

Study the different meanings of each word below, and then read carefully the sentences that follow.  Which meaning does the word have in each sentence?  Write your answers like this:

1. In this sentence "form" means to give form or shape to something.

**form:**   (a)  the shape of something,
        (b)  a long seat,
        (c)  a special paper on which you have to write answers to questions,
        (d)  to give form or shape to something.

1. I am trying to *form* this clay into a dish.
2. Jane had to fill up a *form* before she could join the library.
3. The electric lights were made in the *form* of candles.

**plot:**   (a)  the plan or main story of a play or novel,
        (b)  to plan secretly,
        (c)  a small piece of ground.

4. In this *plot* I am going to grow potatoes.
5. The play at the Royal Theatre has a very exciting *plot*.
6. The prisoner began to *plot* his escape.

**spring:**  (a)  to jump,
        (b)  a strip of metal bent or coiled up,
        (c)  a place where water comes up out of the ground,
        (d)  the season of the year between winter and summer.

7. There is a broken *spring* in this chair.
8. The water from the *spring* was always clear and cold.
9. Tony *sprang* to his feet and ran away.

Now write out three meanings of **hold** in the same way; then write three sentences (10 to 12) using the word with each of these meanings.

# Unit 9 Find the Information

| | |
|---|---|
| Hurrel David, 3 Whiteside Avenue | 091-665 1341 |
| **Hurst Car Rental,** 1 Leith Square | 091-226 7997 |
| Hurst Dr J. R., Sherwood House, Upford | 091-552 7503 |
| Hurst Ronald, 19 Brighton Crescent | 091-229 5454 |
| Hush Mrs A. N., 29 Broom Road | 091-555 2569 |
| Hush Charles, 171 Wilson Street, Upford | 091-346 8315 |
| Hutchinson, William, 13 Windsor Street, Bramton | Bramton 431 |
| Hutchinson W. S., 4 Redland Drive | 091-442 7396 |
| **Hutchinson Sports Centre —** | |
| (Bookings) London Road | 091-556 3914 |
| (Canteen) London Road | 091-556 3917 |

Here is part of a telephone directory. Look at it carefully and write answers to the questions below.

1. What is the telephone number of Mrs Hush?
2. Whose car rental firm is in Leith Square?
3. What is their telephone number?
4. You want to talk to a boy called Richard Hutchinson. You don't know his exact address, but you know he lives in Bramton. What number do you ring?
5. What is the address of Charles Hush?
6. You want to get hold of Dr Ronald Hurst. Which number do you ring?
7. You want to book a badminton court at the sports centre. Which number do you ring?
8. Whose telephone number is 091-442 7396?
9. Who lives in Brighton Crescent?

# Unit 10 Find the Objects

Do you know how to find square 2D? You look along line 2 until you come to column D; that square is 2D. There is a giraffe in square 2D. Now try to answer each of these questions with a complete sentence.

1. What is there in square 4E? (*Begin:* There is a book in ...)
2. What is there in 1B?
3. What is there in square 3F?
4. What is there in 4B?
5. What is in 1F?
6. What is in 2E?
7. In which square is the bicycle? (*Begin:* The bicycle is in ...)
8. In which square is the tree?
9. In which square is the guitar?
10. In which square is the helicopter?
11. In which square is the girl?
12. Is the ice cream in square 3C or 3F?

# Unit 11 Robinson Crusoe

Robinson Crusoe set sail for Africa, but the voyage ended in disaster.   The ship was wrecked, and everyone on board was drowned except Crusoe.   He was washed ashore on an island where no one lived.

Next day Crusoe saw the wreck of the ship lying quite near the shore.   By making himself a raft, he managed to reach the wreck.   He brought ashore all the food and useful things he could find.

Then he set about making himself a home on the deserted island.   He found a cave in the cliff side.   He extended the cave by making a tent of a sort.   After that he built a strong fence right round to protect himself from wild animals.

At the same time he made plans for feeding himself. He found wild grapes and other fruit on the island.   He planted wheat and rice which he had found on board ship, and so grew crops.   He trapped wild goats and soon had a flock of his own to milk.

For nearly twenty years Crusoe lived without hearing another human voice.   His chief friends were a dog, which was the only living thing saved from another wreck on the island, and a parrot.   To cheer himself up Crusoe taught the parrot to talk.   But even the parrot could not prevent his feeling very lonely.

Below are three sentences about each of the first four paragraphs. Write out the sentence that best sums up each paragraph.

A sentence that sums up a paragraph must include all the facts. Notice that in No. 1, the first sentence does not tell us where the shipwreck happened, therefore it does not sum up the whole paragraph. Nor does the third sentence sum up everything, because it does not tell us what kind of island it was, or how Crusoe came to be in the sea. Does the second sentence include practically everything?

1. Robinson Crusoe was shipwrecked.
   Crusoe was shipwrecked on an uninhabited island.
   Robinson Crusoe was washed ashore on an island.

2. Robinson made an excellent raft on which to visit the wreck.
   He saw the wreck near the shore and decided to visit it.
   He reached the wreck on a raft and brought away many useful things.

3. He made a cave bigger by adding a tent to it.
   He made himself a home protected by a strong fence.
   The fence protected him from wild animals.

4. He fed on wild fruit, his own crops and his own goats.
   He grew his own crops from wheat and rice taken off the wreck.
   He trapped a flock of wild goats to provide himself with milk and meat.

5. Write your own sentence to sum up the last paragraph.

# Unit 12 Change the Words

Rewrite each of the following sentences in the way suggested.

1. I am going shopping for my mother.   (Change *I* to *he* and make any other necessary changes.)

2. You have finished your work earlier than you thought you would.   (Change *You* into *I* and make any other necessary changes.)

3. My brother was chasing the cat out of his room.   (Change *brother* to *brothers* and change the rest accordingly.)

4. Today John is not feeling very well.   (Change *Today* to *Yesterday* and make the other changes.)

5. Yesterday the shops were closed and we could not go shopping.   (Make this happen today.)

6. It is raining today and Mr Jackson cannot dig the garden. (Change this so that it happened last Wednesday.)

7. Sara is feeling very proud as she has won the prize for jumping.   (Rewrite this in the past tense.)

8. The boy's books are all on the desk.   (Make *boy's* plural.)

9. The little boy's mother looked surprised.   (Rewrite this without using the apostrophe.)

10. The woman's paper was carried by her dog.   (Make everything plural.)

11. The joiner made this bookcase.   (Rewrite this, beginning: This bookcase was made ...)

12. The bricklayer built this wall.   (In the same way, rewrite this in the passive voice.)

# Unit 13 A Book Collection

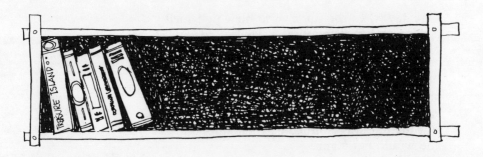

Kathleen is collecting a little library of her own. So far she has five books. Yesterday she arranged them on her shelf. On the left of the bookshelf she placed *Treasure Island* by R. L. Stevenson. Next to this she placed *Tom's Midnight Garden* by Philippa Pearce. After that she placed *Alice in Wonderland* by Lewis Carroll. Then in between *Tom's Midnight Garden* and *Alice in Wonderland* she squeezed *The Little House On The Prairie* by Laura Ingalls Wilder. At the end of the row she placed *Black Beauty* by Anna Sewell.

1. Draw a picture of Kathleen's bookshelf and on it draw the five books. Draw the books big enough so that you will be able to answer the next question.

2. The back of a book that looks out at you from the shelf is called the spine. On the spine of each book write the title of the book.

3. Who is the author of *Tom's Midnight Garden*? (*Begin:* The author of this book is ...)

4. Who is the author of *Alice in Wonderland*?

5. Is *Tom's Midnight Garden* or *Black Beauty* at the extreme right of the row?

6. Between which two books is *Alice in Wonderland*?

7. What book by Laura Ingalls Wilder did Kathleen own?

8. Which book did she put in the middle of the row?

# Unit 14 Man Overboard!

One day when the trade wind blew pell-mell
a sleeping-bag flew into the swell –
Herman grabbed for it – in he fell!
     "Man overboard!" they cried.
"Get hold of the steering blade!"   He tried
and missed.   And Thor went cold with fear
and ran to fetch the safety gear.
But the line was jammed on the bamboo drum
and would not come.
Then Erik threw him a belt – in vain,
for the brute wind blew it back again.
Thrashing the air, lashing the wave,
Herman swam with a wild despair.
But the raft sped on apace –
no swimmer could ever win that race,
and a raft won't tack or steady or brake
for all that a human life's at stake.
If the tide would turn!   If the wind would drop!
But soon he was floundering far astern,
now hid in the hollow, now pitched and tossed
from crest to crest.   They thought him lost
when suddenly Knut plunged in with the line
and life-belt on his arm – oh, fine!
First one was hidden and then the other;
at last they saw two heads together,
a belt, two clinging arms.   They cheered
and waved.   Herman was saved.
Then Erik and Thor and Danielsson
hand over hand hauled them in.

           From *The Ballad of Kon-Tiki* by Ian Serraillier

This is an extract from a poem about the Kon-Tiki expedition in which six men sailed 6400 km across the ocean in a frail balsa-log raft, to prove that people living in A.D. 1100 could have done the same journey in the only craft they knew.

Try to think out answers to the questions on the next page,

and then compare your answers with those listed below in the wrong order. Write out the answers in the same order as the questions they answer.

1. How did Herman fall into the sea?
2. How did the crew first suggest he should save himself?
3. Why could they not use the safety gear?
4. Why was it useless to throw the life-belt to Herman?
5. What is meant by "no swimmer could ever win that race"?
6. Why did the crew not turn back and pick up Herman?
7. Which words show that the crew feared it was all over with Herman?
8. How was Herman rescued in the end?

(a) They could not use it because it was jammed on the bamboo drum.
(b) They suggested he should grasp the steering blade.
(c) They could not do so, because a raft cannot be stopped or turned round.
(d) He fell in when he was reaching for the sleeping bag that had been blown overboard.
(e) This means that no swimmer could ever overtake the raft.
(f) He was saved by Knut who dived in with the life-belt tied to a long line.
(g) Their fear is shown by the words, "They thought him lost".
(h) It was useless because the wind blew it back.

9. Read the extract again, and then write the story of it in three paragraphs:
   (i) Herman falls overboard.
   (ii) All efforts at rescue fail.
   (iii) Knut at last finds a way.

# Unit 15 Opposites

Write out the two sentences in each group that have opposite meanings.

1. (a) John did not speak a word.
   (b) John kept his word.
   (c) John broke his promise.

2. (a) The food was as dull as ditchwater.
   (b) The food was quite uneatable.
   (c) The food was very tasty.

3. (a) Susie was an excellent fiddler.
   (b) Susie felt as fit as a fiddle.
   (c) Susie felt ill.

4. (a) The house is a long way from the stone quarry.
   (b) The house is within a stone's throw from where we are standing.
   (c) The house is a great distance from here.

5. (a) The match will not be played till tomorrow.
   (b) Postpone the match till tomorrow.
   (c) Do not put off the match till tomorrow.

6. (a) The rascal was as bold as brass when he was caught.
   (b) The rascal threw his shoes away when he was caught.
   (c) The rascal shook in his shoes when he was caught.

7. (a) Sobia made light of her friend's mistake.
   (b) Sobia threw light on her friend's mistake.
   (c) Sobia made a great fuss about her friend's mistake.

8. (a) The islanders had made many good wells.
   (b) The islanders were well off.
   (c) Those living on the island were poverty-stricken.

# Unit 16 Write the Story

Write out this story of an Arab and his camel, choosing the correct words from the brackets.

As an Arab sat in his (hotel, tent, school) one cold night, he saw the flap gently lifting. Presently the face of his (horse, cow, camel) looked in. "It is (cold, hot, warm), master. Let me put my (tail, head, hump) inside the tent," pleaded the camel.

"Do so by all means," (replied, asked, inquired) the Arab. So the camel put his head inside the warm tent.

After a moment or two the camel (answered, replied, asked), "May I warm my neck a little too?"

"(Yes, No), by all means," (commanded, ordered, answered) the kind Arab. So the camel put his (head, neck, legs) inside the tent.

It was not (long, short) before the camel spoke again. "It will take only a little (less, more) room for my forelegs. May I not put them in?" So the Arab moved up and made room.

"May I not come right (outside, inside)?" (replied, inquired, repeated) the camel. "I am keeping the tent (shut, closed, open) by standing like this." So the Arab (squeezed, spread, sprawled) himself into a corner and the camel came right into the small tent.

"I see that there is not room for both of us," (asked, observed, replied) the camel by and by. "You are the (smaller, bigger, taller); so it will be better for you to step outside." Saying this, the camel pushed the (cruel, selfish, good) Arab out into the cold.

23

# Unit 17 Sort the Titles

Here are six kinds of books.   Give each its correct definition.

**biography:**         a story written to be acted on the stage
**autobiography:**     an imaginative composition written in verse
**drama:**             an account of one's experiences when visiting places
**poetry:**            the written story of a person's life
**travel:**            any story in prose about imaginary people and events

**fiction:**           the story of a person's life, written by that person

Now make a heading of each of the above kinds of books and then write out each of the following book titles under the correct heading.   There should be three titles under each.

*Shakespeare's Life and Art* by Peter Alexander
*My Own Story* by Emmeline Pankhurst
*Three Short Plays* edited by Richard Hendry
*My Kind of Verse* edited by John Smith
*A Full Life* by Sir Brian Horrocks
*The Riddle of the Painted Box* by Malcolm Saville
*Olivia* by Olivia
*Four Sherlock Holmes Plays* by Michael and Mollie Hardwick
*Flora Thompson* by Margaret Lane
*A Winter in Arabia* by Freya Stark
*Book of Verse for Boys and Girls* edited by J. C. Smith
*Alice in Wonderland* by Lewis Carroll
*In Ethiopia with a Mule* by Dervla Murphy
*Collected Poems* by John Betjeman
*Captain Cook* by R. T. Gould
*Holidays in France* by Roger Savage
*Macbeth* by William Shakespeare
*Treasure Island* by Robert Louis Stevenson

# Unit 18 Using a Dictionary

> **dictate** *v.* 1 to say or read aloud for another person to write down or record. 2 to command or give orders firmly.
> **dictionary** *n.* a book listing words in alphabetical order with their meanings.
> **die** *v.* 1 to cease living. 2 to wither.
> **diesel** *n.* 1 an engine using diesel oil.
> 2 a locomotive driven by a diesel engine.
> **diet** *n.* 1 the kind of food normally eaten by a particular person, community or animal.
> 2 a set course of food, usually arranged for medical reasons.

If we want to use a dictionary we must make sure first of all that we can arrange words in alphabetical order. It is quite simple. If the words begin with different letters, we arrange them according to the first letter. Thus *cricket* comes before *football* because *c* comes before *f* in the alphabet. If the words begin with the same letter we arrange them according to the second letter. Thus *team* comes before *train* because *e* comes before *r*. If the second letters also are the same we must arrange them according to the third letter; and so on. Thus *train* comes before *tram* because *i* comes before *m*, and *diesel* comes before *diet* because *s* comes before *t*.

1. Why does *train* come before *tram*?
2. Why does *Donald* come before *Duncan*?
3. Why does *attention* come before *attraction*?

Arrange each of the following lists in alphabetical order:

4. Peter, Adam, Isobel, Alec, Simon, Ruth
5. London, Melbourne, Birmingham, Bordon, Perth, Garston, Guildford
6. trick, track, truck, trend, trouble, trying
7. show, shot, shall, shift, sheet, shut, shout, shy, shiver, sharply, shopping, shallow.

# Unit 19 Guide Words

In order to find a word in the dictionary you must not only know the alphabet but be able to use guide words. These words are printed at the head of the page. The one on the left tells you the first word given on that page, and the one on the right tells you the last to be given.

Guide words help to tell you at a glance whether or not a word is on the page. You will see how to use them by looking for a word, for example *mound*.

1. As the word begins with *m*, which is in the middle of the alphabet, begin by opening the dictionary in the middle.
2. After you have found the words beginning with *m*, suppose you turn to a page with the guide words **made** and **mark**. You will know that *mound* is not on that page, because *mou* does not come between *mad* and *mar*. Should you turn on or back?
3. You turn on several pages and come to the guide words **moat** and **moss**. You must still turn on, because *mou* comes after *mos*.
4. You turn on and find the guide words **muddy** and **mystery**. You have now turned too far, because *mou* comes before *mud*.
5. You turn back and find the guide words **motor** and **mud**. You know at once that *mound* will be on this page, because *mou* comes after *mot* and before *mud*.

Now try to answer these questions:

1. If the guide words are **motor** and **mud**, why will *mustard* not appear on that page?
2. If the guide words are **moat** and **moss**, why will *mole* appear on that page?
3. If the guide words are **prosper** and **publication**, say which five of these words will appear on that page: *proverb, puzzle, public, pulpit, progress, protest, print, pry, prow.*

# Unit 20 A Book Review

*Worzel Gummidge* was the first of Barbara Euphan Todd's now famous stories of Gummidge, the scarecrow. It tells the story of how John and Susan came to know him. They were staying on a farm after having had whooping cough. One afternoon they went for a walk in Ten-acre Field and there discovered the scarecrow. He did seem a bit different from most scarecrows, but they thought no more about him. That evening, when the farmer and his wife were out, John went off to bed. Then, as Susan sat by the fire, who should walk into the room but the scarecrow! He introduced himself as Gummidge, and from that day the children's acquaintance with Gummidge was to lead them into some very awkward situations and provide them with some very funny moments. Anyone who likes a story of children's adventures, told with humour and filled with interesting facts about life in the country, will enjoy *Worzel Gummidge*. The book is attractively produced.

1. Who is the author of *Worzel Gummidge*? (*Begin:* The author of this book ...)
2. What is the name of the scarecrow?
3. Who, besides Gummidge, are the main characters in the story?
4. Where did the children first see Gummidge?
5. From what illness were John and Susan recovering?
6. Write out the sentence in which we first discover that Gummidge is alive.
7. How do we know that *Worzel Gummidge* is a humorous story as well as exciting?
8. Write a review, like this one, suggesting a book you have recently read and enjoyed.

# Unit 21 The Witch's Cat

Gobbolino had caught three mice by the time the cook came downstairs, but she would not look at him or give him a word of praise.

She set about making gruel for   1   orphans' breakfast. It was very thin   2   grey and tasteless, and the orphans   3   it. The porteress had told the   4   to make them good porridge, but   5   never got up herself until the   6   were cleared. So the lazy cook   7   gruel day after day, and the   8   knew nothing whatever about it.

When   9   saw the unpleasant grey mixture that   10   cook was stirring in her cauldron   11   felt sorry for the orphans, and   12   her back was turned he put   13   spell on the gruel that filled   14   full of sugar-plums.

From *Gobbolino the Witch's Cat*
by Ursula Moray Williams

Read this passage carefully.   You will see that there are numbers in several places where there should be words.   See if you can guess which words the author would have used.   Then make a list of them with their numbers in your book.

# Unit 22 Crunchy Biscuits

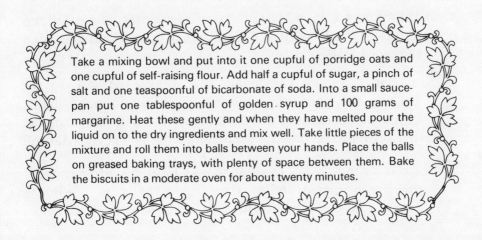

Take a mixing bowl and put into it one cupful of porridge oats and one cupful of self-raising flour. Add half a cupful of sugar, a pinch of salt and one teaspoonful of bicarbonate of soda. Into a small sauce-pan put one tablespoonful of golden syrup and 100 grams of margarine. Heat these gently and when they have melted pour the liquid on to the dry ingredients and mix well. Take little pieces of the mixture and roll them into balls between your hands. Place the balls on greased baking trays, with plenty of space between them. Bake the biscuits in a moderate oven for about twenty minutes.

1. Read the recipe for making crunchy biscuits and then write out the following instructions in the same order as you are told to perform them in the recipe.

   Add the sugar, salt and bicarbonate of soda.
   Melt the syrup and margarine.
   Mix the oats and flour.
   Add the liquid to the dry ingredients.
   Place the balls on baking trays.
   Bake the biscuits in a moderate oven.
   Form the mixture into little balls.

2. Answer these questions in simple but complete sentences.
   (a) Why do you have to grease the baking trays?
   (b) Why do you have to leave plenty of space between the little balls?
   (c) Would it be easy or difficult to make these biscuits?

# Unit 23 Some Puzzles for You

1. If the figures 1, 2, 3, 4, 5, 6, 7, in that order, stand for the letters of the word PICTURE, what figures will stand for the word RIPE?

2. Ron Baker, Gerry Gardener, and Trevor Mason do the baking, the gardening and the building in our village. None, however, does the work connected with his surname. If Ron Baker is not the gardener, what is Trevor Mason?

3. Peter is as tall as his brother would be if his brother were three centimetres taller than he actually is. Who is shorter, Peter or his brother?

4. Susan is younger than Jane who is older than Jessica. Jessica's younger sister Laura is older than Susan. How many of the girls named are older than Laura?

5. A packet of Omy is dearer than a packet of Ome, and a packet of Ome is cheaper than a packet of Ono. Which is the cheapest?

6. It rained on Tuesday. I know this because two of the following statements are true. Which two are they?
   (a) The last time it rained was yesterday.
   (b) It snowed on Monday.
   (c) It rained two days ago.
   (d) It will be Thursday tomorrow.

7. Twelve matches are arranged like this. Which two matches would you move to make seven squares? Describe which matches you would move and where you would put them. (Solution on page 94.)

# Unit 24 The Ant and the Dove

One day an ant, while quenching its thirst at a spring, fell into the water and was almost drowned. A dove that happened to be perched on a tree nearby saw the ant's danger and, plucking off a leaf, let it fall into the water just in front of the ant. The ant climbed on to the leaf, and in a few minutes was blown safely to dry land.

At the very moment the ant landed, a man who was out hunting wild birds was spreading his net ready to trap the dove. The ant, seeing what the man was about to do, bit his heel. The bite gave the man such a start that he dropped his net. Meanwhile, the dove was aroused to a sense of her danger and flew away to safety.

1. Write out the sentence that tells us about the kind action the dove did for the ant.

2. Write out the sentence that tells us what the ant did in kindness toward the dove.

3. A fowler is a man who traps wild birds. Write out the sentence that tells us that the dove escaped from the fowler.

4. Which of these is the moral that this fable teaches? Write it out.
   (a) Look before you leap.
   (b) Slow but sure wins the race.
   (c) One good turn deserves another.
   (d) A bird in the hand is worth two in the bush.

5. Imagine that the ant can speak. Write out the story as the ant might have told it. You could begin like this:
   One day, while I was quenching my thirst at a spring, I fell into the water and was almost drowned . . .

# Unit 25 Which are Correct?

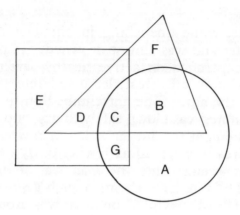

Six of these statements about the diagram are correct, and four are incorrect. Write out the correct ones only, and number them 1 to 6.

(*a*) D is in the square only.

(*b*) A is in the circle only.

(*c*) D is in the triangle and the square.

(*d*) B is in the circle and the triangle.

(*e*) C is not in the circle or the triangle.

(*f*) D is the only letter not in the circle.

(*g*) E and A are the only letters not in the triangle.

(*h*) E is not in the circle or the triangle.

(*i*) G is in the square and circle but not in the triangle.

(*j*) C is in all three figures.

Now answer these questions with complete sentences.

1. Which letter is in the circle only?

2. Which letter is in the triangle only?

3. Which letter is in the triangle and circle but not in the square?

4. Which letter is in all three figures?

5. Which letter is in the square and circle but not in the triangle?

6. Which letters are in one figure only?

# Unit 26 The Road to School

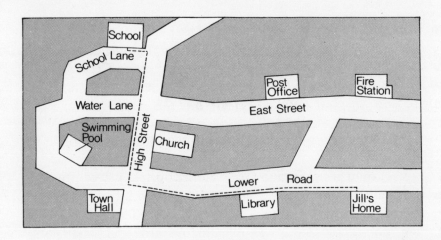

1. The dotted line shows the quickest way from Jill's home to her school. This is how she describes how to get from her house to the school. Choose the right words and write out the complete description.

   When I go out of the front gate, I turn (left, right) and walk along (Lower Road, East Street) till I come to the (first, second) turning on the (left, right). This is called (School Lane, High Street). I walk up High Street till I come to the (first, second) turning on my (left, right). This is called (Water Lane, School Lane). I go up School Lane till I come to the school on my (left, right).

2. Copy out the street plan, missing out the dotted line. Put in a dotted line to show the quickest way from the fire station to the church. Then write out the directions for walking to the church from the fire station.

3. Put in a dotted line to show the way from the library to the school if you have to call at the swimming pool on the way. Then write out directions for reaching the school from the library by way of the swimming pool.

# Unit 27 Classifying

Can you put things in their right class? You are first given the names of three things that all belong to one class. You are then given the names of three more things. You have to choose the one of these that belongs to the same class, and give your reason for your choice. *Begin like this:*

1. I choose bungalow, because it is another dwelling.

| | |
|---|---|
| 1. house, mansion, cottage | floor, bungalow, ceiling |
| 2. red, yellow, pink | paint, pencil, blue |
| 3. carrot, marrow, swede | potato, garden, flower |
| 4. dog, pony, cow | farm, stable, cat |
| 5. peach, pear, plum | apple, leek, onion |
| 6. aunt, cousin, sister | dentist, farmer, mother |
| 7. Sunday, Monday, Tuesday | January, Wednesday, Christmas |
| 8. February, March, April | Thursday, Easter, July |
| 9. rose, daisy, violet | tomato, apple, lilac |
| 10. crow, sparrow, chaffinch | rabbit, bee, robin |
| 11. trout, salmon, cod | chips, steak, sardine |
| 12. Peter, John, Bruce | Alice, Margaret, George |
| 13. walnut, lime, beech | pine, stick, toffee |
| 14. car, motor bike, lorry | aeroplane, bus, camel |
| 15. Helen, Anna, Jane | Sharon, Peter, Michael |
| 16. cup, saucer, dish | spoon, fork |

# Unit 28 The Golden Egg

The greedy man was not content with only one egg at a time. It laid a golden egg every day. There was once a man who owned a wonderful goose. "There must be many golden eggs inside that bird," he said to himself. In this way he killed the goose, and from that day there were no more golden eggs. The moral is that people who try to get too much sometimes lose what they have. So he cut open the goose, hoping to obtain many eggs at once.

1. Set out the sentences above in their right order. By doing this you will have written the fable of the goose that laid the golden eggs.
2. A fable is a story made up to teach some lesson, or moral as we call it. What lesson does this one teach?
3. Why was the goose called wonderful?
4. Why was the man called greedy?
5. Did this story ever really happen?
6. There is another fable, about a dog and his reflection, that teaches the same moral. If you know it, write it out. If not, write out any fable you know.

# Unit 29 What to Do in an Emergency

Below are some instructions for carrying out first aid in certain cases. Look at the examples in the box, then write a sentence telling which set of instructions you should follow in each case. *Begin like this :*

    1. This is what should be done in the case of a foreign body in the eye.

| | | |
|---|---|---|
| **drowning** | **burns** | **fracture of limb** |
| **choking** | **fainting** | **foreign body in the eye** |

1. If you can see the cause of the trouble, pull down the lower lid and try to remove the cause with the moistened corner of a clean handkerchief.
2. Bathe the affected part at once with cold water and continue to do this for at least ten minutes. Then cover it with a clean, dry cloth. Do not bandage it tightly or apply oils.
3. Let the patient sit down and bend forward until his head hangs down between his knees.
4. Let the patient lean his head forward; then thump his back. If it is a small child, hold him upside down across your arm or bent knee and then thump his back.
5. Clear the patient's mouth of weeds and water, loosen clothing at the neck, and then apply artificial respiration.
6. Until a doctor is found, keep the limb from moving. The best way of doing this is by fastening it firmly to the body. Tie an injured leg to a good leg, or fasten an injured arm across the chest. Pad any hollows with folded cloth, socks, etc. Do not move the injured person.

# Unit 30  A Book Review

How would you like to spend the summer holidays on an island in a lake?  If the idea appeals to you, you are sure to enjoy reading *Swallows and Amazons* by Arthur Ransome.  His story is about four children who were allowed to camp on Wild Cat Island.  They called themselves the Swallows, because their boat was called *The Swallow*. They referred to each other as Captain John, Able Seaman Titty, Mate Susan, and Ship's Boy Roger.  The Amazons were two girls, Peggy and Nancy, whom they met on the island.  They all became friends, and the adventures that befell them and the open-air life they led will keep you interested for many hours.  Arthur Ransome knew his sailing, camping and outdoor life at first hand and tells about them in a lively and exciting way.

1. Who is the author of *Swallows and Amazons*?  (*Begin*: The author of "Swallows and Amazons" is ...)
2. What was the island in the lake called?
3. Who was called the Mate?
4. At what time of the year did these events take place?
5. Why did some of the children call themselves the Swallows?
6. Was Peggy a Swallow?
7. Which sentence tells the reader that the author had himself sailed boats?
8. Write a similar review of any book you have recently read, recommending it to others.

# Unit 31  What Does He Do?

A certain Mr Brown was once staying at a seaside camp site. All the children there wanted to know what he was, for they liked the man very much.  One morning Sue asked him outright what he did for a living.  "I sometimes make people's hair look nice," replied Mr Brown.

"Then you are a hairdresser?" said Sue.

"Oh no, I am not.  I sometimes brush clothes."

"I know," said Peter, "you are a dry-cleaner!"

"Oh dear, no," said Mr Brown.  "Sometimes I make coats, trousers or dresses."

"I see," said Kevin, "you are a tailor."

"No.  I make boots and shoes, you see."

"Ah, then you are a shoemaker," suggested Sobia.

"I am not a shoemaker, for you see I often make faces," and Mr Brown made such funny faces that everyone laughed.

"I've got it," shouted Judy.  "You are a comedian!"

Then Mr Brown said, "You are all wrong; but everything I said is true, because I am a portrait painter."

Read the story opposite carefully.   Then see if you can finish these sentences correctly.   The endings, in the wrong order, are given in the second list.   Write out the complete sentences.

1. The children wanted to know what Mr Brown was
2. Sue thought he must be a hairdresser
3. Peter thought the man must be a dry-cleaner
4. Judy thought he must be a comedian
5. Sobia argued that he must be a shoemaker
6. Kevin thought Mr Brown was a tailor
7. Really, he did all these things

(a) because he brushed clothes.
(b) because he was a portrait painter.
(c) because he made boots and shoes.
(d) because he could make such funny faces.
(e) since he made clothes.
(f) for they were very fond of him.
(g) as he made people's hair look nice.

Now answer these questions with complete sentences.
   *Begin like this:*
      8. She thought he was . . .

8. Why did Sobia think he was a shoemaker?
9. Why did Judy imagine Mr Brown was a comedian?
10. Why did Kevin suppose he was a tailor?
11. Why did Sue believe he was a hairdresser?
12. Why did Peter think the man must be a dry-cleaner?
13. What did Mr Brown do for a living?
14. Explain in what sense Mr Brown could claim to make people's hair look nice.

39

# Unit 32 News at Last

Old Anchor Inn<br>
Bristol<br>
1st March 17—.

Dear Livesey,

The ship is bought and fitted. She lies at anchor, ready for sea. You never imagined a sweeter schooner – two hundred tonnes; name, *Hispaniola*.

I got her through my old friend, Blandly. The admirable fellow literally slaved in my interest, and so, I may say, did everyone in Bristol, as soon as they got wind of the port we sailed for – treasure, I mean.

It was the crew that troubled me. I wished a round score of men – in case of natives, buccaneers or the odious French – and I had the worry of the deuce itself to find so much as half a dozen, till the most remarkable stroke of fortune brought me the very man that I required.

I was standing on the dock, when, by the merest accident, I fell in talk with him. I found he was an old sailor, kept a public-house, knew all the seafaring men in Bristol, had lost his health ashore, and wanted a good berth as cook to get to sea again. He had hobbled down there that morning, he said, to get a smell of the salt. I engaged him on the spot to be ship's cook. Long John Silver, he is called, and has lost a leg.

Well, sir, I thought I had only found a cook, but it was a crew I had discovered. Between Silver and myself we got together in a few days a company of the toughest old salts imaginable. Long John even got rid of two out of the six or seven I had already engaged. He showed me in a moment that they were just the freshwater swabs we had to fear in an adventure of importance.

I am in the most magnificent health and spirits, eating like a bull, sleeping like a tree, yet I shall not enjoy a moment till I hear my old tarpaulins tramping round the capstan. Seaward ho! Hang the treasure! It's the glory of the sea that has turned my head. So now, Livesey, come post; do not lose an hour, if you respect me.

John Trelawney

1. Find these words in the letter, and then pair each one with its correct definition.

   (a) **schooner:**   sea-robber or pirate
   (b) **literally:**   machine for winding cable
   (c) **buccaneer:**   word for word, without exaggeration
   (d) **odious:**   sleeping place on board; sea job
   (e) **berth:**   hateful
   (f) **capstan:**   a ship with two or more masts and fore and aft sails

2. By whom and to whom was the letter written?
3. Where was the correspondent staying when he wrote the letter?
4. What was the size of the *Hispaniola*?
5. For what purpose had the ship been bought?
6. Why did everyone in Bristol work hard for Trelawney?
7. How many men did Trelawney want for his crew?
8. Why did he want a rather large crew?
9. This letter is taken from a story called *Treasure Island* by R. L. Stevenson, in which Long John Silver is the villain. He has heard about the treasure and intends to get it himself. How did he make his meeting with Trelawney appear accidental?
10. Why, do you think, was he so keen to supply the crew?
11. Why did he get rid of two of those already engaged?
12. The letter was written a long time ago, and some of its expressions are now old-fashioned. Pick out any two such expressions and state what we should say today instead.

# Unit 33 A Family History

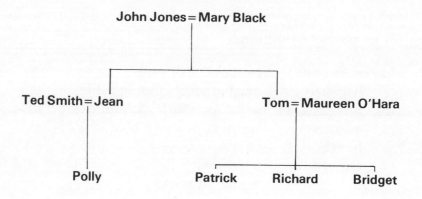

Can you read this family tree? It is quite simple. The signs mean that John Jones married Mary Black and they had two children. Their son Tom married Maureen O'Hara, and their daughter Jean married Ted Smith, and so on.

Now answer each of these questions with a complete sentence. *Begin like this:*

    1. They had three children.

  1. How many children did Tom and Maureen Jones have?
  2. Whom did John Jones marry?
  3. How many children did John and Mary Jones have?
  4. What was their son's name?
  5. What was their daughter's name when she became married?
  6. Whom did Tom Jones marry?
  7. Whose daughter was Bridget Jones?
  8. What were the names of Bridget's two brothers?
  9. Who was one of Patrick Jones's uncles?
10. Who was Polly Smith's mother?
11. Who was Maureen Jones's niece?
12. Who was Jean Smith's niece?

# Unit 34 The Pasture

I'm going out to clean the pasture spring;
I'll only stop to rake the leaves away
(And wait to watch the water clear, I may):
I shan't be gone long. – You come too.

I'm going out to fetch the little calf
That's standing by the mother.    It's so young
It totters when she licks it with her tongue.
I shan't be gone long. – You come too.

Robert Frost

1. What is a pasture?    Try to think of any other words meaning
   pasture.
2. The word "spring" has several meanings.    Write a list of
   any you can think of.
3. Which meaning has it in line 1?    How do you know?
4. Why would the water not be clear?
5. Why should the calf totter when the cow licks it?
6. Do you think Robert Frost would really be away for only
   a short time?
7. Have you ever said "I shan't be long" and been away a long
   time?    Write two sentences about it.

43

# Unit 35 Regions

Read these descriptions carefully and compare them with the pictures on the opposite page.   In this way make up your mind which region is being described.   Then draw a picture of each region, give it a title and write out the description of it below.

This region is so cold that it is always buried under snow and ice.   In the winter there is no sunshine, for the sun never rises above the horizon.   The days and nights are then one long period of dim twilight.   In the summer the sun shines all day and all night, but it is never very high in the sky and gives neither warmth nor much light.   Winter or summer, it is always bitterly cold, so that only a few bears or penguins can remain alive.

In this region there is little or no rain, so that farming can be carried on only where underground water comes to the surface to form oases.   At midday the heat of the sun is terrific, but at night it can be very cold.   For kilometre after kilometre there is nothing but bare rocky ground or stretches of sand dunes dotted with a few cactus plants.

The earth's surface here rises everywhere to lofty peaks and bare ledges of rock.   The highest caps and ridges are always covered with snow, though down lower the snow melts in summer.   Then torrents rush downwards in foaming water- falls.   Sheep graze on the lower slopes, and in the sheltered valleys cattle are reared.

The land in this region is low-lying and near the equator. The weather is always hot and moist.   Nearly every day there are torrential showers, after which the sun comes out again and the air seems hotter and steamier than ever.   There are great muddy rivers running through thick growths of jungle.

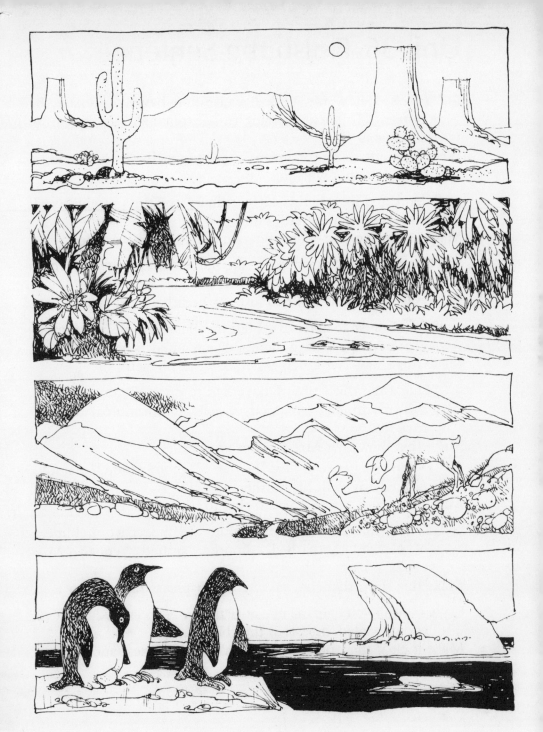

# Unit 36 Finish the Sentence

1. "You see, it won't work because you haven't pressed the button," (chuckled, laughed, explained, shouted) the mechanic.
Write this out so that it means that the mechanic was giving a reason for its not working.

2. "Come and look at this extraordinary creature," (whispered, shrieked, stammered) Tom.
Make this mean that Tom spoke in a loud, piercing voice.

3. "For goodness sake don't make me laugh any more," (muttered, explained, gasped, ordered) Liz.
Make this show that Liz had lost her breath.

4. "Now I must go and see if I left my glasses in the bathroom," Uncle (gasped, thought aloud, screamed, whispered).
Make this show that Uncle was talking to himself.

5. "That's the third time I have had to open the door for you this morning," (snapped, chuckled, mumbled, argued) Mrs Jay.
Make this show that Mrs Jay was cross.

6. "Do go and get ready for the party," (commanded, grunted, coaxed, giggled) his mother.
Make this show that she was trying to persuade him.

7. "That is not the sort of behaviour we expect from children of eleven," (breathed, shouted, sniffed, replied) Miss Cross.
Make this show that she was slightly displeased.

8. "Couldn't you help me just once more?" (exclaimed, pleaded, asked, wailed, asserted) the child.
Make it clear that the child was making an earnest appeal.

# Unit 37 Crosswords

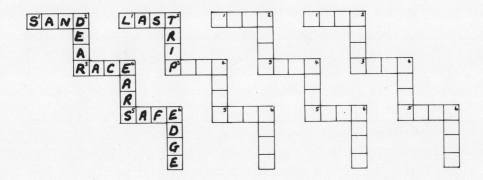

This is a special kind of crossword puzzle. It's like going down a staircase. The first puzzle has been filled in. The second one has been started. The clues are given below. Try to finish it. In the same way solve the third puzzle with the help of the clues below. You can fill in the fourth one in whatever way you like. When you have done so, supply your own clues for solving it.

## CLUES FOR SECOND PUZZLE

*Across*

1. The opposite of first.
3. Another name for a bucket.
5. Information about something that has happened.

*Down*

2. To catch a person's foot to throw him down.
4. With little or no fat.
6. In a short while.

## CLUES FOR THIRD PUZZLE

*Across*

1. You smell with this.
3. Long narrow woven strip of cotton.
5. 365 days.

*Down*

2. The direction opposite west.
4. The opposite of difficult.
6. A building that has fallen to pieces.

# Unit 38 Could It Happen Now?

Below is a list of actions. If the action could not have taken place several hundred years ago, say so. If the action was more likely to have happened several hundred years ago than today, say so. Make your answers like this:

    1. Carrying cargo by a sailing boat is more likely to have happened several hundred years ago than today.

    2. Steering a modern car could not have happened several hundred years ago.

  1. Carrying cargo by a sailing boat
  2. Steering a modern car
  3. Speaking over the telephone
  4. Shooting game with a bow and arrow
  5. Roasting chicken in front of an open fire
  6. Travelling to Spain by aeroplane
  7. Sailing in a motor boat
  8. Flying faster than sound
  9. Crossing the sea in submarines
 10. Switching on an electric light
 11. Going into battle on a horse
 12. Living in caves
 13. Dying of the plague
 14. Being held up by a highwayman
 15. Watching a play on television
 16. Salting down meat for use during the winter

# Unit 39 They Mean the Same

---

(*a*)  "Has my friend called for me?" asked Martin.
(*b*)  "May I switch on TV, Mum?" asked Martin.
(*c*)  "It is going to be hot," said Martin.
(*d*)  "Surely I can't have lost it?" said Martin.
(*e*)  "How hot it is!" said Martin.
(*f*)  "Thank you, Auntie; it's exactly what I want," said
    Martin.

---

The six sentences in the box mean the same as the six sentences below, but they are in a different order. Write them in the same order.

1. Martin asked his mother if he could switch on TV.
2. Martin exclaimed that it was very hot.
3. Martin thanked his aunt and told her it was exactly what he wanted.
4. Martin inquired if his friend had called for him.
5. Martin felt sure that he could not have lost it.
6. Martin declared that the weather would be hot.

When we give the actual words spoken, we call it *direct speech*. All the sentences in the box are direct speech. But when we report what was said without giving the actual words, we call it *reported speech*. All the sentences in the first list are reported speech. Write the following as direct speech:

7. Susan said she was going into the town.
8. John asked if he might go to the cinema.
9. Jane exclaimed that it was a very beautiful sight.
10. George asked Bruce if he had any brothers.

# Unit 40 Look Alive!

The Curator was showing some schoolchildren round his museum in London, when they came to a pair of human skulls. "Now I want you to look at these," he said.

"What are they?" asked John.

"They are the two skulls of Captain Cutlass, the notorious pirate," replied the Curator, wanting to make sure that his audience continued to pay attention. "This small one is Captain Cutlass as a boy of ten, while the bigger one is the skull of the same man when he died in battle off the coast of Sussex."

The Curator paused. There was a long silence, and then one of the children woke up.

"That can't be right," said Susan. "Even a pirate can only die once."

1. Is this story meant to be serious, exciting or amusing?
2. Why did the Curator play a trick on the children?
3. Why is it quite impossible to have in the museum a skull of Captain Cutlass as a boy of ten?
4. Which adjective in the story means "well known for being bad"?
5. Write the last two sentences in reported speech.
6. Study the punctuation of the story, and then state what happens every time there is a fresh speaker.
7. Write out the following story giving it its right paragraphing and punctuation:

   a singing lesson was in progress you must try to sing louder than that Jill said the teacher but I'm singing as loudly as I can said Jill rather hurt well try to throw yourself into the singing more yes open your mouth wide and throw yourself into it

# Unit 41 Good Manners

Write a sentence in answer to each question.  *Begin like this:*
   1. It would be more polite to make light of them.

1. Should you laugh at other people's mistakes, or try to make light of them?
2. When visitors call should you leave them standing, or offer them chairs?
3. Should you allow yourself to get cross when someone teases you, or try to laugh it off?
4. When you are beaten in a game should you let yourself get annoyed, or try to look cheerful?
5. Should you talk while the film is showing, or wait till the interval?
6. Should you help yourself to cake first, or pass it to the others first?
7. Should you ask to be allowed to pass, or push your way past people?
8. Should you say "I and Mary" or "Mary and I"?
9. Should you offer your seat to elderly people, or let them stand?
10. Is it courteous to slam the door behind you, or to close it quietly?

# Unit 42 Telling a Story

MARCH HARE: I vote the young lady tells us a story.

ALICE [*rather alarmed at the proposal*]: I am afraid I don't know one.

MARCH HARE: } Then the Dormouse shall! Wake up, Dormouse!
MAD HATTER: } [*They pinch it on both sides at once.*]

DORMOUSE: [*Slowly opens his eyes*] I wasn't asleep. [*In a hoarse, feeble voice*] I heard every word you fellows were saying.

MARCH HARE: Tell us a story!

ALICE: Yes, please do!

HATTER: And be quick about it, or you'll be asleep again before it's done.

DORMOUSE [*beginning in a great hurry*]: Once upon a time there were three little sisters, and their names were Elsie, Lacie, and Tillie; and they lived at the bottom of a well – .

ALICE [*always interested in questions of eating and drinking*]: What did they live on?

DORMOUSE [*after thinking a moment or two*]: They lived on treacle.

ALICE [*gently*]: They couldn't have done that, you know; they'd have been ill.

DORMOUSE: So they were; *very* ill.

The above extract is written in the form of a play. Rewrite it as if it were in story form. *Begin like this :*

"I vote the young lady tells us a story," said the March Hare.

"I'm afraid I don't know one," replied Alice, rather alarmed at the proposal.

# Unit 43 Advertisements

**Brown Burmese cat** urgently requires good home with scope for adventure. Phone Benford 5621 after 6 p.m.

**Waitress**, experienced, requires post in town. Own bedroom, 37-hour week. Write Mary Jenkins, 45 Elm Grove, London SW3 9PG.

**Hayling Island.**
Dinner, bed and breakfast. A few vacancies left for June and September. Jackson, Sea View Hotel, Beach Road.

Two bricklayers wanted. Apply Tall & Sons, Builders, 24 New Road, Bridgeport.

*Ford Escort*, 1978. 4-door, red, excellent condition. Write Box 751.

1. Which advertisement would you expect to find under each of these headings in the newspaper?
    (a) Situations Vacant
    (b) Holiday Accommodation
    (c) Cars for Sale
    (d) Situations Wanted
    (e) Pets for Sale
2. What kind of animal is for sale?
3. Who wants two bricklayers?
4. What is the Jacksons' hotel called?
5. What kind of position does Mary Jenkins want?
6. When could you have a holiday at Sea View Hotel?
7. How would you find out who is selling the car?
8. What kind of home would the cat probably like?
9. You have something to sell, such as a dog, pigeon, tennis racket or bicycle. Write out the advertisement you would send to the local paper.

# Unit 44 More Puzzles for You

1. If Simon is taller than Earl, and Trevor is the tallest of the three, who is the shortest?

2. Maria is as old as Sharon would have been two years ago if Sharon had not been a year older. Which is the elder child?

3. Kevin, Peter, Lesley and Sue are brothers and sisters. All of them can swim, except Lesley. Only Kevin and Lesley can ride a horse. Kevin is the only one who cannot play tennis. Peter and Lesley can play the piano well, but the others cannot.
   (a) Which three things can Lesley do?
   (b) Which of the children can do three of the things mentioned?
   (c) Which of them can do only two of the things?
   (d) Which things can Sue do that Peter can do?

4. Which day in December is as far from January 1st as January 12th is in the following month?

5. If all monkeys are vegetarians, say which two of the following statements are not true:
   (a) Some monkeys may eat nuts.
   (b) No monkey is an eater of flesh.
   (c) Monkeys in Scotland eat rats.
   (d) Many monkeys like bananas.
   (e) A few monkeys are carnivorous.

# Unit 45 Primroses

You will find primroses growing in all parts of the United Kingdom, though they are more abundant in the south. In an average season the primrose flowers in March, but in mild weather it is often found in flower as early as February in southern England. Indeed, clumps of primroses in a sheltered part of my garden in Surrey have occasionally broken into flower before Christmas and continued to show a few blooms right through the winter. The primrose is by nature a woodland flower and gives of its best under the protection of trees.

1. When do primroses usually come into flower?
2. Where do primroses grow most plentifully?
3. In what sort of surroundings do they grow best?
4. Do they flower earlier in the north or south of the country?
5. Do they ever flower in December?
6. Why would you expect to find at least some primroses in Staffordshire?
7. Where does the writer of this passage live?
8. Which word in the paragraph means the opposite of "scarce"?

# Unit 46 Fill in the Blanks

Read the meanings of the three words in each section. Then write out the sentence below them, using the three words to fill the blanks.

**population:** total number of inhabitants
**occupation:** a person's employment
**engineering:** the planning and building of machines

1. The —— of a great part of the —— of Coventry is ——, since several car manufacturers have factories there.

**atlas:** a collection of maps
**map:** a drawing showing the earth's surface or part of it
**boundary:** border or edge (of a country etc)

2. In the —— we found a —— of France, whose southern —— touches Spain.

**climate:** general weather conditions
**temperature:** the degree of heat or cold
**rainfall:** the amount of rain that falls

3. England has a pleasant ——, because the —— is rarely uncomfortably high or low, and even in winter the —— is rarely heavy enough to cause floods.

**natives:** persons born in a certain country are natives of that country
**inhabitants:** persons who live in a certain place
**immigrants:** persons who come into a country to live

4. Many of the —— of Australia were —— of Britain who went to Australia as —— seeking a better living.

# Unit 47 Which Sentence?

A good paragraph deals with one topic and one only. No sentence that is not about that one topic should be included in the paragraph. In each of the following paragraphs there is one sentence that is not about the topic. Find it and write it out.

1. Robins are friendly birds. When I am digging in the garden it is never long before a robin comes near me. It will peck at worms almost within arm's reach. Robins do not leave Britain in the winter. Sometimes they will even eat out of my hand.

2. When travelling at speed, the kangaroo can hop great distances. At walking pace, so to speak, its hop is only a metre long, but the length of the hop increases with its speed. A fast-moving kangaroo can cover as much as six metres at a hop. The mother kangaroo carries her baby in a pouch.

3. A punt is a shallow flat-bottomed boat with square ends. It is moved by a pole which the punter pushes against the bed of the river. Some rivers have trees overhanging them. There is usually room for at least four people to sit down in a punt.

4. Donald is a big boy for his age. His father is a bus-driver. He has fair hair and blue eyes. Though rather tall, he is not ungainly. His movements are quick and almost graceful. He has a way of using his hands that reminds one of his mother.

# Unit 48 Describe the Children

forgetful   courteous   thrifty   helpful
selfish    obedient    untidy   ungrateful
      meddlesome   generous

Choose the right word to describe each person mentioned below and use it in a sentence to describe that person. *Begin like this:*

 1. Sobia was a thrifty girl.

1. Sobia opened a savings account at the Post Office. Every Saturday she paid in the pound she earned by helping her uncle in the shop.
2. Angus assisted his mother by laying the table and washing up the dinner dishes.
3. James left his toys scattered over the floor and his books lying on the chair.
4. When she saw that Mrs Elder had no seat, Angela offered to give her hers.
5. Karen grabbed her present and ran off without saying, "Thank you".
6. Tom always did what he was told.
7. Charles liked to interfere in other people's affairs.
8. Sara offered to give half her sweets to her friend.
9. William bought some crisps but did not give his friend any.
10. Azzah could never remember to bring her book.

# Unit 49 Topic Sentences

1. Norway is a land of mountains.
2. Unlike Norway, the coast of the Netherlands is made up of sand dunes.
3. Southern Italy is much warmer than either Norway or the Netherlands.

Each of these sentences is the opening of a paragraph. Each one indicates very clearly what the paragraph is about. We call this kind of sentence a *topic sentence*, because it tells what the topic of the paragraph is. Write out the first topic sentence and add four sentences to it from the list below, so that you make a complete paragraph. Then do the same with the second and third topic sentences.

(*a*) It is a narrow strip of land stretching south into the Mediterranean.
(*b*) The coast is broken and rocky, and the mountains often rise precipitously from the shore.
(*c*) Beyond the sand dunes live the Dutch people.
(*d*) But their homes are on land that is lower than the sea beyond the dunes.
(*e*) There the winter is never very cold.
(*f*) Along the coast are numerous rocky islands.
(*g*) So the dunes really hold back the sea.
(*h*) Between these islands and the shore is a long deep waterway.
(*i*) In the summer it is hot, and hardly a drop of rain falls.
(*j*) To make sure the sea doesn't break through, the Dutch have reinforced the dunes with dykes made of stone and concrete.
(*k*) Vineyards and olive groves flourish in this warm climate.
(*l*) Here the water is calm and safe for ships.

Now write three similar paragraphs about the Swiss mountains, the African jungle and the French Riviera.

# Unit 50 What Do They Mean?

(a)  Ann was a girl you would call *impetuous*.

(b)  Ann was always rushing to do things without thinking what she was doing, so we called her *impetuous* Ann.

If you did not know the meaning of the word *impetuous* you could not find it from (a), could you?   It might mean anything in that sentence; but in (b) it can only mean that Ann was hasty and rash.

In each of the following pairs choose the sentence in which the meaning of the italicised word is clear.

1. (a)  The *laboratory* is next to the Director's office.
   (b)  The scientists do their work in a well-equipped *laboratory*.
2. (a)  Brian went to the *dentist* to have a tooth filled.
   (b)  Brian goes to the *dentist* every six months.
3. (a)  Mr Mumble is always *inaudible* wherever he speaks.
   (b)  Mr Mumble spoke so softly that he was *inaudible* at the back of the hall.
4. (a)  This story is the most *humorous* I have ever read.
   (b)  I laughed all through this *humorous* film.
5. (a)  I start my holidays a *fortnight* from today.
   (b)  I shall be away from home during the *fortnight* of August 1st to 14th.
6. (a)  This *reliable* child will never let you down once he has undertaken to do something.
   (b)  Peter is the most *reliable* boy in the school.
7. (a)  His scribbled message was very hard to read as his writing is almost *illegible*.
   (b)  I find John's writing very nearly *illegible*.

# Unit 51 Sun, Moon and Earth

The earth is round. It rotates on its own axis once every 24 hours, so giving us night and day. It goes round the sun and completes its orbit in just over 365 days. It is therefore one of the sun's satellites.

The moon, revolving round the earth and completing its orbit in about 29 days, is the earth's satellite. It seems to shine, but in fact its light is merely reflected from the sun. It is very much smaller than the earth.

The sun looks much bigger than the other stars, but this is only because it is much nearer than any of the others. It is about 153 million kilometres away, whereas the next nearest star is about 40 thousand billion kilometres away. Actually, compared to most of these distant stars the sun is quite tiny, although it is vastly bigger than the earth.

1. Find these words in the paragraphs above and match each with its correct definition:
   - (a) **rotate:**    a heavenly body that moves round a larger one
   - (b) **axis:**    a thousand times a million
   - (c) **orbit:**    to go round or revolve
   - (d) **satellite:**    the line round which a thing turns
   - (e) **billion:**    the path followed by one heavenly body round another
2. Why does the sun seem bigger than other stars?
3. Roughly how often does the earth go round the sun?
4. Where does the moon's brightness come from?
5. How can you tell that the sun is bigger than the moon?
6. Find these words in the passage, and write sentences like those on page 60, to make their meaning clear:
   - (a) reflect  (b) distant  (c) rotate  (d) orbit

# Unit 52 Definitions

**inscription:** writing on an article such as a gift or a medal

**limerick:** a humorous poem of five lines, with the first line beating: ti TUM ti-ti TUM ti-ti TUM

**proverb:** a short wise saying containing a widely recognised truth

**public notice:** an announcement in writing for the benefit of the public

**receipt:** a written and signed statement that something, e.g. money, has been received

**riddle:** a puzzling question to which the answer is cleverly funny

**tongue twister:** a saying, usually humorous, which is difficult to say quickly

**weather forecast:** an announcement indicating what the weather is likely to be

Read the definitions above. Then write out the sentences below in this order:

1. a riddle
2. a tongue twister
3. an inscription
4. a receipt
5. a weather forecast
6. a public notice
7. a proverb
8. the first line of a limerick

(a) There was a young lady from Ryde.

(b) This seat was presented by John Atkins.

(c) ROAD CLOSED. ALL TRAFFIC TURN LEFT.

(d) Sixty-six silly souls sitting on sticks shyly shot stacks of sticky snails.

(e) Take care of the pence and the pounds will take care of themselves.

(f) Why is the letter f like a banana skin?

(g) Tomorrow it will be sunny and warm, with a light breeze.

(h) Received with thanks from J. Banks the sum of £1.77. Signed: Robert Morris.

# Unit 53 Draw the Island

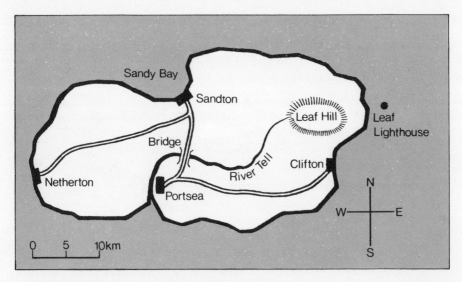

1. Copy this map into your book.
2. Mark on it Lone Farm half way between Netherton and Sandton on the north side of the road.
3. On the south side of the road from Portsea to Clifton, 2 kilometres out of Clifton, mark the Island Hospital.
4. Colour the sea and the river blue, the roads red and the hill brown.
5. Into the River Tell, 5 kilometres from its source, runs a stream from a lake 5 kilometres north. Put in the lake and the stream and colour them blue.
6. How far is it from Clifton to Portsea as the crow flies (i.e. in a straight line)?
7. How far is it from Netherton to Portsea by road?
8. Is Netherton on the east or west side of the island?
9. Is the lighthouse east or west of the island?
10. Draw another map of an imaginary island and put in a river, a mountain, two villages, three roads, a bridge and a castle. Supply a scale and the points of the compass.

# Unit 54 The Brave Baron

Read the first paragraph of this absurdly wonderful story of
Baron Munchausen. Choose and write out the sentence below
it that tells what the *whole* paragraph is about. Do the same
with the other paragraphs.

One day I was travelling through the
forests of Poland, when a fierce and
terrible wolf rushed suddenly upon me.
At that time I had neither sword nor
pistol. There was not even a stick with
which I could defend myself.

(*a*)  The Baron was making a journey.

(*b*)  Baron Munchausen had no means of defending himself
in the forest.

(*c*)  The defenceless Baron was attacked by a wolf in the forest.

I had no time to think of a plan, and
as the wolf sprang upon me, I thrust
my fist into his open mouth. I pushed
so hard that my arm went into his body,
right up to my shoulder!

(*d*) The Baron nearly lost his arm.

(*e*) Without thinking, the Baron drove his hand into the wolf's mouth right up to his shoulder.

(*f*) The Baron could not think what to do as the wolf attacked him.

Now what was I to do? If I pulled out my arm, the wolf would fly at me more angrily than before. If I did not pull it out, my position would be just as difficult. For a moment I stood facing those flaming eyes. Then quickly I took hold of the wolf's tail, and turned him inside out like a glove. I flung him to the ground, left him there, and continued on my journey.

(*g*) After that, the Baron saved himself by turning the wolf inside out like a glove and going on his way.

(*h*) After that, the Baron scarcely knew what to do next.

(*i*) After that, Baron Munchausen stood looking at the angry wolf, till he flung him to the ground and continued his journey.

# Unit 55 A Nature Diary

*2nd January*. The snowdrops in Mum's window-box are showing their flowers.

*14th January*. I saw the first primrose of the year in a sheltered corner of the park. This morning in the playground it was wet and cold.

*24th January*. We hung some bacon rind and peanuts outside our classroom window, and bluetits perched on them, pecking skilfully at the nuts.

*18th February*. Snow quite deep today. We could see the footprints of several birds, as well as a wandering cat, outside the school. Our feet made good prints too.

*1st March*. The shops are selling bunches of daffodils, but there are none growing in the ground here yet.

*15th March*. A blustery day with clouds moving fast across the sky.

*8th April*. Some blackbirds have built a nest in the hedge around the park. I hope no one will steal the eggs.

*19th April*. We watched a television programme about sheep and lambs. A girl was feeding an orphan lamb with a bottle of milk.

*4th May*. The sun was shining all day and we felt quite warm in the playground this morning. In the evenings it is not so dark, and the birds are still singing when I go to bed.

Read the entries in the nature diary opposite, then write answers to these questions.

1. How did the bluetits peck the nuts?
2. On what date did the writer see tne first primrose?
3. Where did the blackbirds build their nest?
4. On what date did the children watch a television programme?
5. Why did the lamb need to be fed by bottle?
6. Did much snow fall on the 18th February? How do you know?
7. Were the snowdrops in flower before the primrose?
8. Where did the children hang the food for the birds?
9. Why did the writer hope to keep the blackbirds' nest a secret?
10. Why would the birds be quiet in the evening in the winter?
11. Turn back to page 49 and then write these sentences in reported form.
   (a) "I have just found a robin's nest," said Tony.
   (b) "Did you see that wonderful TV programme investigating the intelligence of birds?" Jane asked Ali.
   (c) "Yes", replied Ali, "how intelligent some of those birds were!"
   (d) "Tom, do you know that badgers are so intelligent that they sometimes take their bedding out of the sett and air it in the sun?" asked Peter.

# Unit 56 How to Find Out

Do you always know where to look for the information you need? Use the following material to write a series of sentences like this:

    1. The find the meaning of a word, consult a dictionary.

| *To find* | *consult* |
|---|---|
| 1. the meaning of a word | a joke book |
| 2. the shortest road from one town to another | a calendar |
| 3. the position of a country | a road map |
| 4. a funny story | an atlas |
| 5. the arrival of the next train | a dictionary |
| 6. the date | a telephone directory |
| 7. someone's telephone number | the menu |
| 8. the second course of a meal in a restaurant | the timetable |

Now use this material to write a series of sentences beginning like this:

    9. To find out what is wrong with your tooth, consult a dentist.

| *To find out* | *consult* |
|---|---|
| 9. what is wrong with your tooth | the doctor |
| 10. why your chest aches | the grocer |
| 11. the price of herrings | a dentist |
| 12. the price of marmalade | a weather vane |
| 13. the cost of sending a parcel | the librarian |
| 14. the way to make a cake | the fishmonger |
| 15. the author of a book | a post office clerk |
| 16. the direction of the wind | a recipe book |

# Unit 57 Hiawatha

Out of childhood into manhood
Now had grown my Hiawatha,
Skilled in all the craft of hunters,
Learned in all the lore of old men,
In all youthful sports and pastimes,
In all manly arts and labours.
Swift of foot was Hiawatha;
He could shoot an arrow from him,
And run forward with such fleetness
That the arrow fell behind him!
Strong of arm was Hiawatha;
He could shoot ten arrows upwards,
Shoot them with such strength and swiftness
That the tenth had left the bow-string
Ere the first to earth had fallen!

From *Hiawatha* by H. W. Longfellow

1. Which line tells us that Hiawatha had benefited from the wisdom of his elders?
2. How do we know that he was good at tracking wild animals?
3. How do we know that he was good at games?
4. Explain in your own words how the poet shows that Hiawatha was a fast sprinter.
5. How does the poet show that Hiawatha had a very strong arm?
6. Here is a way of showing the beat of words in a line:

   Shoot them / with such / strength and / swiftness

   Can you do the same for the last two lines of this poem?

# Unit 58 Write Some Limericks

Can you write limericks? The lines missing from those listed below are given first. Decide where each line belongs, and then write out the complete limericks.

> By simply not dotting his *i*'s.
> Returned from her college down south.
> There is less in your brain
> For a wheel off her skate
> There was a young lady of Diss,
> This no more will she state
> He saves litres of ink

1. A boastful young schoolgirl of Louth
   . . . . . . . . . . . . . . . . . . . . . . . . . . . . . .
   Her mother said, "Jane
   . . . . . . . . . . . . . . . . . . .
   Than ever came out of your mouth."

2. There's a very mean man of Belsize,
   Who thinks he is clever and wise.
   And what do you think?
   . . . . . . . . . . . . . . . . . . .
   . . . . . . . . . . . . . . . . . . .

3. . . . . . . . . . . . . . . . . . . . . . . . . . . . . .
   Who said, "I think skating is bliss."
   . . . . . . . . . . . . . . . . . . .
   . . . . . . . . . . . . . . . . . . .
   Made her finish up something like this.

# Unit 59 They Mean the Same

Pair each adjective phrase on the left with one of similar meaning on the right.   *Begin like this:*

    1. despised by all: scorned by everyone

| | |
|---|---|
| 1. despised by all | loved by everyone |
| 2. with his hat askew | whitened in the sunlight |
| 3. adored by all | dotted with wreckage |
| 4. littered with jetsam | with his hat crooked |
| 5. bleached by the sun | wearing one's smartest clothes |
| 6. dressed up to the nines | scorned by everyone |

Do the same with these adverb phrases:

| | |
|---|---|
| 7. in a great hurry | as a joke |
| 8. in jest | with much haste |
| 9. at the last moment | in the gathering dusk |
| 10. in the open air | with wonderful nimbleness |
| 11. in the twilight | out of doors |
| 12. out of the blue | with tireless force |
| 13. with marvellous agility | at the eleventh hour |
| 14. with indefatigable energy | without warning |

Then do the same with these noun phrases:

| | |
|---|---|
| 15. an enticing odour | strange gestures |
| 16. a sacred promise | absolute trust |
| 17. weird signs | a tempting smell |
| 18. an uncared-for look | football clothes |
| 19. soccer gear | an unkempt appearance |
| 20. implicit faith | a solemn undertaking |

# Unit 60 Fun on the Beach

They worked rapidly, and by the time the boat was due had built quite a high mound. Patricia explained that the wash would not come until a few minutes after the boat had gone by, and as soon as she had passed they all climbed on to the mound and waited expectantly. Very soon the first wave broke; it was quite small, but behind it came a bigger one and very quickly in succession, three more, bigger still. The mound was surrounded, and the children, all clinging together, kept their footing with difficulty on the shifting pebbles as the receding waves sucked them back.

"They're not big waves at all today," said Patricia disappointedly, but she spoke too soon. The last and biggest wave of the wash suddenly joined forces with an ordinary wave, a rush of water swirled up the beach, demolished the mound completely and plunged them all, stumbling and hurting their feet on the shifting stones, well over their knees in water. But all this was as nothing compared with the sad plight of Mrs Watkins! Happily murmuring "purl, plain, purl," she had glanced up to see what the children were doing, and beheld the sea, which she had supposed going out, advancing in a huge wave towards her! Before she could get to her feet, the water was up to her, under her, over her, all round her, and receding again, taking with it her knitting instructions, most of the tea, and Kate Ruggles' precious hat!

From *The Family From One End Street* by Eve Garnett

Find these words in the extract, and then give each its right meaning.

1. **mound:**    going backward
2. **expectantly:**    tripping by striking the foot against something
3. **succession:**    tore down completely
4. **wash:**    a firm position of the feet
5. **footing:**    waves caused by the passage of a ship
6. **receding:**    as if looking forward to something
7. **swirled:**    a series one after the other
8. **demolished:**    moved with a twisting motion
9. **stumbling**    an unfortunate state or condition
10. **plight:**    a heap of earth or stones

Now answer the questions.

11. How do we know that the mound was made of pebbles? (*Answer:* We know this because the author says that the children standing on the mound had difficulty in keeping their footing on the shifting pebbles.)
12. How do we know that Mrs Watkins was knitting when the big wave reached her?
13. How do we know that Mrs Watkins was sitting when the wave reached her?
14. How do we know that the children were going to have a picnic tea on the beach?
15. How do we know that Kate thought a lot of her hat?
16. How do we know that Patricia was hoping the waves would be big ones?

# Unit 61 How People Live

Study these definitions carefully, and then answer the questions on the opposite page.

(a) A landlord is a person who owns a house and lets someone else live in it in return for rent.

(b) Rent is the sum of money that a tenant pays the landlord for the right to live in one of his houses.

(c) The tenant is the person who has the right to live in a house belonging to someone else, to whom he pays rent.

(d) A lodger is a person who lives with another family in exchange for a sum of money. He or she probably has a room alone and has meals with the family.

(e) A detached house is one that stands on its own, not joined to any other house.

(f) A semi-detached house is one that is joined to another house on one side but not on the other.

(g) A bungalow is a house with a floor on the ground level only.

(h) A flat is a set of rooms on one floor only, usually in a large house with several floors.

(i) An estate agency is a firm that sells houses on behalf of the owners.

Sara Jones pays fifteen pounds a week rent.   The landlord is Mr Beaumont.

1. Who therefore receives the fifteen pounds?
2. Who is the tenant?
3. Who owns the house?

Helen Green lives in a set of rooms on one floor of a large house. Mrs White lives in a little house that has only one floor.   Colin Brown lives in a modern house that has no other house joined to it.   Trevor Pink owns a house that has another joined to it on one side only.

4. Who lives in the bungalow?
5. Who lives in a detached house?
6. Who has a semi-detached house?

Mary Jenkins bought No. 15 New Street.   She let it to John Davies who pays a rent of £20.50 a week.   Now she has asked Dowse & Co. to try to sell the house for her.

7. Who is the tenant of No. 15 New Street?
8. Who is the landlord?
9. Who has been receiving the rent?
10. What is the name of the firm of estate agents?

Tony Single lodges with Mr and Mrs Blank.   He pays fifteen pounds a week for his board (food) and lodging.   Mr Blank does not own his house but pays his landlord a rent of twenty pounds a week.

11. Who is the lodger?
12. Who receives fifteen pounds a week?
13. Who receives twenty pounds a week?

# Unit 62 The Escape

In the fall of the year, when the days were shortening and the bite of frost was coming into the air, White Fang got his chance for liberty. For several days there had been a great hubbub in the village. The summer camp was being dismantled, and the tribe, bag and baggage, was preparing to go off to the fall hunting. White Fang watched it all with eager eyes, and when the tepees began to come down and the canoes were loading by the bank, he understood. Already the canoes were departing, and some were disappearing down the river.

Quite deliberately he determined to stay behind. He waited his opportunity to slink out of camp to the woods. Here, in the running stream where ice was beginning to form, he hid his trail. Then he crawled into the heart of a dense thicket and waited.

The time passed by, and he slept intermittently for hours. Then he was aroused by Grey Beaver's voice calling him by name. White Fang trembled with fear, and though the impulse came to crawl out of his hiding-place, he resisted it. After a time the voice died away, and some time after that he crept out to enjoy the success of his undertaking.

From *White Fang* by Jack London

Find the following words in the extract on the opposite page and pair each with its definition.

1. **fall:** tents of the American Indians
2. **hubbub:** bushes growing close together
3. **dismantled:** awakened or stirred to action
4. **tepees:** autumn
5. **deliberately:** off and on
6. **thicket:** strove against
7. **intermittently:** confused noise or disturbance
8. **aroused:** sudden inclination or desire
9. **impulse:** after careful thought
10. **resisted:** pulled down or taken to pieces

Now answer the questions.

11. At what time of the year did White Fang escape?
12. What caused the hubbub in the village?
13. "He understood." What did White Fang understand?
14. How did he get his chance to escape?
15. Where were the tribe going?
16. How did White Fang hide his trail?
17. Did he sleep while he was lying hidden?
18. How do we know that White Fang was missed?
19. What was White Fang's "undertaking"?
20. If you did not know that "fall" meant autumn, how could you tell from the first paragraph?
21. Which sentence shows that the author gives White Fang the power of thought?
22. Which three words show that he did not answer the call of Grey Beaver?
23. Think out what this extract is about. Then write a single sentence to sum it up.

# Unit 63 Look It Up

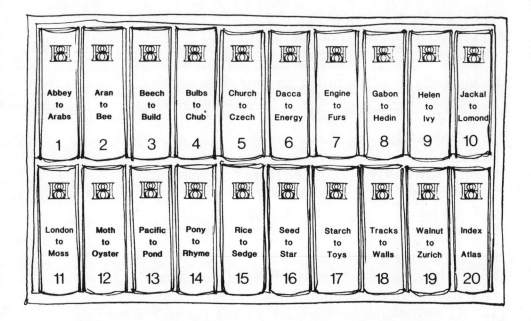

Here is a set of encyclopaedias. On the spine of each book there is the number of the volume and the first and last word in each. Volume 20 contains an atlas and the index to the whole set. Answer each of the questions with a complete sentence.
*Begin like this:*

1. I could read about moths in Volume 12.

1. In which volume could you read about moths?
2. Where would you find out about Australia?
3. Which volume would tell you what nomads are?
4. In how many volumes would you find words beginning with **s**?
5. You have been asked to make a list of the countries in South America. Which volume would help you with this?
6. Make a list of three things that might be in Volume 6.
7. What do you think the index would tell you?

# Unit 64 Proverbs

1. When Peter went out he always allowed his friend to pay for him.
2. Jane was a very ill-mannered girl.
3. Lester was a boy who was inclined to give up hope too soon.
4. Angela chattered too much.
5. Bruce was far too daring.
6. Wherever Sue went she always arrived late.
7. Azzah did not stick to one task or job for long.
8. Mary was for ever talking of the wonderful things she would do when she had earned a pile of money.
9. John would never take a risk.
10. Anne was terribly upset by the loss of her pet rabbit, and refused to be cheered up.

Which of the proverbs listed below would you read to each person mentioned above? *Begin your answers like this:*

    1. I should tell Peter that "He who pays the piper calls the tune".

(a) Civility costs nothing.
(b) Look before you leap.
(c) Jack of all trades, master of none.
(d) Nothing venture, nothing win.
(e) Don't count your chickens before they are hatched.
(f) Every cloud has a silver lining.
(g) The early bird catches the worm.
(h) Empty vessels make most noise.
(i) While there's life, there's hope.
(j) He who pays the piper calls the tune.

# Unit 65 A Chase

I waited for no more. I knocked over the candle-stick and ——.
How I got away with a whole skin I know not to this day. I
tore open the —— before his lordship could reach me in the
darkness and confusion, and burst through with such sudden-
ness that I upset the two lackeys, who had been listening at the
——. I probably owed my life to their curiosity, for my way
was then clear to the street. By the time my pursuers had
raised a hue and —— after me I was almost out of their ——.
I had not time to think. Dashing down to the deserted ——,
I plunged into the water and —— out into the darkness. The
hubbub on shore subsided as they scattered in search of me.
Fortunately, nobody had seen me ——. I trod water as I
divested myself of as much of my —— as I could, and then

settled down to the long swim ahead of me. I knew where our boat was —— and was pretty sure I could reach her. The water was bitterly cold.

From Blow the Man Down by Charles Vipont

1. Write out the extract using these words to fill the blanks.

| | | | | |
|---|---|---|---|---|
| **clothing** | **cry** | **door** | **clutches** | **swam** |
| **keyhole** | **fled** | **quay** | **anchored** | **dive** |

Find the following words in your extract and pair each with its right meaning.

2. **lackeys:**     a confused noise or uproar
3. **curiosity:**     grasping hands
4. **pursuers:**     slavish followers
5. **clutches:**     people who follow in order to catch
6. **deserted:**     stripped or freed
7. **quay:**     with everybody gone
8. **hubbub:**     eager desire to know
9. **subsided:**     held in place with an anchor
10. **divested:**     died down
11. **anchored:**     landing place where ships load and unload

12. How do we know that this happened at night? (*Begin:* We know this because ...)
13. How do we know that the lackeys wanted to know what was happening in the room?
14. How do we know that there was no one on the quay?
15. Why do you think he knocked over the candlestick before fleeing?
16. Why do you think he tried to strip off his clothing?
17. What makes you think the writer is a good swimmer?
18. Sum up the extract in a single sentence, beginning: The paragraph tells how the writer ...

# Unit 66 Fables

Here, briefly told, is a selection of fables. Every fable teaches a lesson or moral, as it is called. What moral does each of these teach? The morals are listed at the foot of the opposite page. Write them out in the same order as the fables.

1. A hare and a tortoise once ran a race. The hare raced away at a great pace. He felt so sure of winning that he took a nap half way. He was still asleep several hours later when the tortoise passed the winning post, after plodding along steadily.

2. As a pair of horses pulled a waggon along a rough road, the wheels set up a tremendous creaking. "Brutes!" cried the driver to the wheels. "Why do you groan, when the animals who are doing all the pulling are silent?"

3. One day a fox fell down a well and could not get out. Presently a goat came along and asked the fox if the water was good down the well. "It is delicious," replied the fox. "Come down and try it." So the goat leaped straight in. Immediately the fox jumped upon the goat's back and leaped out, leaving the goat a prisoner in the well instead of himself.

4. A farm worker on his way home one day found a snake half-dead with cold. He took pity on the creature and brought it back to his cottage to revive by the fire. No sooner had the warmth restored the snake, than it started to attack the children in the cottage. The farm worker was then obliged to kill the snake.

5. When a fox met a lion for the first time, he nearly died of fright. When he met him for the second time, he was

still afraid, but he managed not to show it. When he saw him the third time, he ventured to go right up to him and ask him how he was.

6. A donkey was delighted by the sound of some grasshoppers chirping. He wanted to be able to sing like them; so he asked them what they fed on to make them sing so sweetly. When they told him that they fed on nothing but dew, the donkey decided to feed on the same diet. He soon died of hunger.

7. Said an old crab to a young one, "Why do you walk so crooked, child? Walk straight!"
"Mother," said the young crab, "show me the way, will you? When I see you walking straight, I will try to follow."

8. A very thirsty crow was delighted to find a tall jug with a little water in the bottom. But, try as he would, he could not reach the water to drink it. Then he tried to break the jug or knock it over, but he was not strong enough to do either. In the end he noticed some pebbles near by. He dropped a great many of them, one by one, into the jug. This raised the level of the water, so that at last he was able to quench his thirst.

## Morals
(a) Example is better than precept (preaching).
(b) Slow but steady wins the race.
(c) Necessity is the mother of invention.
(d) Those who return evil for good must in the end expect to be ill-treated.
(e) Those who cry loudest are not always the most hurt.
(f) Familiarity breeds contempt.
(g) One man's meat is another man's poison.
(h) Look before you leap.

# Unit 67 People as Animals

We often use the names of animals when we describe people. For example, if we wanted to say that Paul Blank was a deceitful person we might call him a snake in the grass.

Can you now write one sentence about each of the persons named below, using an adjective from the list below instead of mentioning the name of the animal? *Begin like this:*

    1. Henry was very stubborn.

1. I have tried to reason with Henry; but it was no use.   I have never seen such a mule.
2. Donald proved to be a snake in the grass.   He did not keep his promise, and so let me down badly.
3. Here comes Tom, the young monkey who caused all the trouble.
4. Don't do that Jane, you little goose, or you'll break it.
5. Mr Meek is so chicken-hearted, he will never stand up for himself.
6. What has upset Sara Jenkins?   She is like a bear with a sore head this morning.
7. There was something lion-hearted about the way Ian went for the thief.
8. Jill, the little pig, has eaten all the cakes.

| | | | |
|---|---|---|---|
| greedy | deceitful | courageous | mischievous |
| silly | timid | stubborn | ill-tempered |

# Unit 68 The Paper Bill

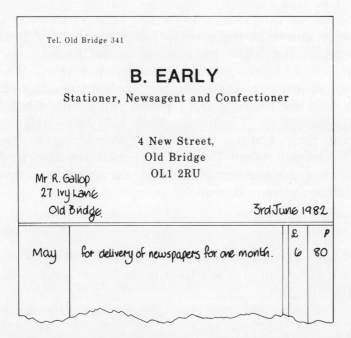

Tel. Old Bridge 341

## B. EARLY

Stationer, Newsagent and Confectioner

4 New Street,
Old Bridge
OL1 2RU

Mr R. Gallop
27 Ivy Lane
Old Bridge.

3rd June 1982

| | | £ | P |
|---|---|---|---|
| May | for delivery of newspapers for one month. | 6 | 80 |

This is the bill that Mr Early, the newsagent, sent to Mr Gallop. Mr Gallop owes Mr Early the amount of money shown on the bill. Can you now answer these questions?

1. How much does Mr Gallop owe Mr Early? (*Begin:* Mr Gallop owes ...)
2. On what date was the bill sent out? (*Begin:* The bill was sent ...)
3. What is Mr Early's telephone number?
4. Where is the newsagent's shop?
5. Where does Mr Gallop live?
6. What is Mr Early besides a newsagent?
7. Name three things you could probably buy at Mr Early's shop in addition to newspapers.
8. For what month were the newspapers delivered?
9. What is a stationer?

# Unit 69 Who Did It?

As soon as the burglars disappeared, Jane Smith rang up the police and told them what had happened. "I was awakened in the night by a noise in the house. As I switched on the light I saw that it was five past two. Then I slipped on my dressing gown and crept downstairs very quietly. In the dining room I found two burglars breaking into my safe. They were both tall dark men, and well past their youth. They were whispering to each other in French when I silently opened the door. As soon as they saw me standing there, they rushed to open the window and jumped out."

1. Jane Smith's neighbour is a man of forty and has very fair hair. How can you tell that he could not have been one of the burglars?
2. On the night of the burglary, Kevin Jones, living on the opposite side of the road, was at a dance. He did not leave the dance till 2.15 a.m. How can you tell that he could not have been one of the burglars?
3. David Lewis was arrested by the police at 2.20 a.m. He was standing in a doorway near Mrs Smith's house, and looked as if he were hiding. He is a tall man aged 45. He can speak no languages but English and a little Welsh. Could he have been one of the burglars? Give your reasons.
4. The police also arrested Ken Morgan for questioning. He was found loitering in a lane behind Jane Smith's house at 2.30 a.m. Ken Morgan has almost black hair, is 180 cm tall, and had his fiftieth birthday the day before the burglary occurred. His mother is French. Do you think he could have been one of the burglars? Give your reasons.

# Unit 70 Sense or Nonsense

Read these sentences carefully.   Each in some way is absurd.
Rewrite each to make good sense.   *Begin like this :*
   1. We put on our raincoats when it rains.

1. We put on our raincoats when the sun shines.
2. Bread is made mostly from flowers.
3. Not a sound could be heard in the noisy room.
4. The empty bag contained a kilogram of apples.
5. The busy workmen sat idly in the sun.
6. A cowboy is a horseman who rounds up sparrows.
7. Along the smooth beach Peter had to pick his way among many rocks, boulders and pebbles.
8. Shortly after sunset, as the sun rose above the hill, Amy began her journey.
9. This mixture consists of water only.
10. The six children lined up in four pairs.
11. My aunt always visits us twice a year, and each visit she stays seven months.
12. Staring into the fire, Jeremy Rounder stood there warming his back.
13. Exactly half of the fifteen candidates are girls.
14. The sum of £10.30 was found on the arrested man, including two five-pound notes and a fifty-pence piece.
15. More women were married last year than men.
16. My sister was married yesterday to a man who trains race-horses in the parish church.
17. The archaeologist dug up an old coin, the age of which he knew exactly because it bore the date of 1626 B.C.

# Unit 71 Look It Up

## Index

| | | | |
|---|---|---|---|
| Age | 30 | Jumping | 17 |
| Aids | 19–22 | Lungeing | 17 |
| Bits | 31 | Mounting | 6 |
| Blacksmith | 10 | Mucking out | 27 |
| Breeds | 31 | Paces | 16–17 |
| Bridles | 13–15 | Reins | 13, 15, 16, 17 |
| Cantering | 16 | Roads | 5 |
| Countryside | 5 | Rugs | 28 |
| Dismounting | 7 | Saddles | 10–13 |
| Feeding | 25–27 | Shoes | 10 |
| Fences | 5 | Spurs | 11 |
| Galloping | 16 | Stables | 26–28 |
| Girths | 12 | Stirrups | 11 |
| Grooming | 28 | Tack | 10–15 |
| Hands | 3 | Trotting | 16 |
| Health | 29 | Vets | 29 |
| Hooves | 30 | Walking | 15 |

Here is the index of a book. You can probably guess it is about horses and ponies. See if you can answer these questions after you have read the index very carefully.

1. Where would you look for information on grooming?
2. Joan's father is buying a pony, but he's not sure how old it is. Where would he find the information he needs in this book?
3. What sort of facts do you think are given on page 5?
4. You will see that there is an entry on "hands". Why is it there? If you don't know, use your dictionary.
5. Which pages of the book deal with the care of horses?
6. A "vet" is an animal doctor. The word "vet" is an abbreviation. Try to find out the full word it stands for.
7. Which is faster, cantering or galloping? Find out from a dictionary.
8. How many pages has the author written on shoeing a horse?
9. John's pony has a cough. Which page should he consult?

# Unit 72  A Serial to Watch

**THE SILVER SWORD**

BY IAN SERRAILLIER

Adapted for television by C. E. Webber
into seven episodes.

Produced by Shaun Sutton

### Episode 3 – The Burning of the City

Ruth Balicki . . . . . . . . . . . . . . . . . . . . . . . . . . . . PAT PLEASANCE
Edek Balicki . . . . . . . . . . . . . . . . . . . . . . . . . . MELVYN HAYES
Bronia Balicki . . . . . . . . . . . . . . . . . . . . . . . INGRID SYLVESTER
Farmer . . . . . . . . . . . . . . . . . . . . . . . . . . . . . . MICHAEL KENT
Black Marketeer . . . . . . . . . . . . . . . . . . . . . GERTAN KLAUBER
Jan . . . . . . . . . . . . . . . . . . . . . . . . . . . . . . . . . FRAZER HINES
Yankel . . . . . . . . . . . . . . . . . . . . . . . . . . . GRAHAM HARPER
Jalna . . . . . . . . . . . . . . . . . . . . . . . . . . . . . . . . JUDY HORN
Ivan . . . . . . . . . . . . . . . . . . . . . . . . . . . . . . COLIN DOUGLAS
Russian Lieutenant . . . . . . . . . . . . . . . . . . . . . TIM HUDSON

1. The script for this television play was adapted from a novel.
   What was the title of the novel?
2. Who adapted Ian Serraillier's novel into a script for television?
3. If one instalment was shown every Sunday, for how many
   weeks did the play run?
4. Which instalment was being shown on this occasion?
5. Judy Horn took the part of Jalna.  What part did Frazer
   Hines play?
6. Ruth, Edek and Bronia are Polish children.  How could we
   guess that the story was about Poland during its occupation
   by the Soviet Union?

# Unit 73 A Quiz

1 There are two letters in the word RATION which have three letters in between them in the alphabet.   Which are they?

2. Sam, Peter and Margaret all like coffee, but Jane doesn't. Cocoa is liked by Sam and Jane but not by the other two. Lemon squash is detested by Sam, but much liked by the others.   The two boys love Coca-Cola as much as the girls hate it.

   (a)  Do any of the children like all four drinks?
   (b)  Which of them like three of the drinks?
   (c)  Which of them dislike two of the drinks?
   (d)  If Peter and Margaret came to your house, which cold drink could you offer them that they would both like?

3. Foxfield lies east of Cowley, and Cowley lies south of Oxley. Jill lives in Foxfield and has to cycle through Cowley in order to go to school at Oxley.   When she gets to Cowley does she have to turn right, turn left, or go straight on?

4. Aytown has no swimming pool but it has a park, a cinema and a theatre.   Beetown has only a cinema and a park. Ceetown has only a swimming pool and a cinema, while Deetown has only a park and a cinema.

   (a)  Which towns have neither theatre nor swimming pool?
   (b)  Which towns are without a swimming pool?
   (c)  What have Aytown and Ceetown in common?
   (d)  Which town lacks a park?

# Unit 74 Tell the Story

Look at these pictures and write in your book the story that they tell.

What do you think happened next? See if you can write an ending to the story.

# Unit 75 Woodlice

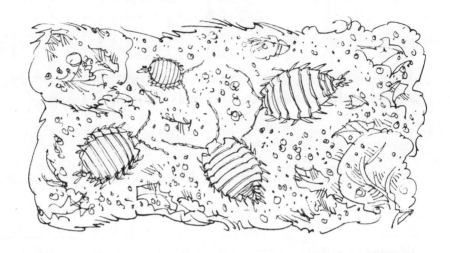

Most crustaceans such as lobsters, crabs and shrimps, live in the sea. Woodlice are one of the few crustaceans that live on the land. They are very common in gardens, where they are unpopular because they eat all kinds of vegetable matter. If you lift up a few damp stones you will see these dumpy animals scurrying about on six pairs of short legs under their protective many-jointed shell. This shell causes the woodlouse a lot of problems. As it grows, the shell becomes too tight and has to be cast off. This moulting occurs about ten times in a lifetime. After the first moult, an extra pair of legs is grown. But if you are lucky enough to see a woodlouse after a moult, you will see how defenceless it is until its new shell is grown. Also look out for the female after mating, when she grows a pouch between her front legs, where first the eggs and then the young stay until the pouch splits. About twenty small white youngsters emerge from the pouch one by one.

From *The Family Scientist* by Judith Hann

1. Find where the following words are used in the account of woodlice on the opposite page, and then give each its correct definition.
   (a) **moulting:**   short and fat
   (b) **pouch:**   running quickly
   (c) **dumpy:**   liked by nobody
   (d) **unpopular:**   pocket for eggs
   (e) **scurrying:**   casting off a too-tight shell

2. The plural of woodlouse is woodlice. Can you think of another word which forms its plural the same way? Can you think of a word ending -*ouse* which does not form its plural this way?

3. Answer each of these questions with a complete sentence.
   (a) Give an example of a crustacean which lives in the sea.
   (b) Where are woodlice usually found?
   (c) What do woodlice eat?
   (d) How many legs do woodlice have?
   (e) How could you describe the woodlouse's shell?
   (f) How many young woodlice are born at a time?

# Acknowledgements

The author and publishers are grateful to the following for giving permission to reproduce extracts from copyright works:

A & C Black Ltd, for an extract from *Victorian Children* by Eleanor Allen; the Estate of Robert Frost and Jonathan Cape Ltd, for 'The Pasture' from *The Poetry of Robert Frost* (edited by Edward Gunnery Latham); William Collins Sons & Co Ltd, for an extract from *Friday's Tunnel* by John Verney; George G. Harrap & Co Ltd, for an extract from *Gobbolino the Witch's Cat* by Ursula Moray Williams; Macdonald Futura, for an extract from *The Family Scientist* by Judith Hann; Frederick Muller Ltd, for an extract from *The Family from One End Street* by Eve Garnett; and Ian Serraillier for part of *The Ballad of Kon-Tiki* (from *The Windmill Book of Ballads* published by Heinemann Educational Books).

Solution to puzzle 7 on page 30.

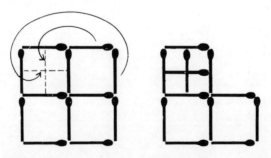